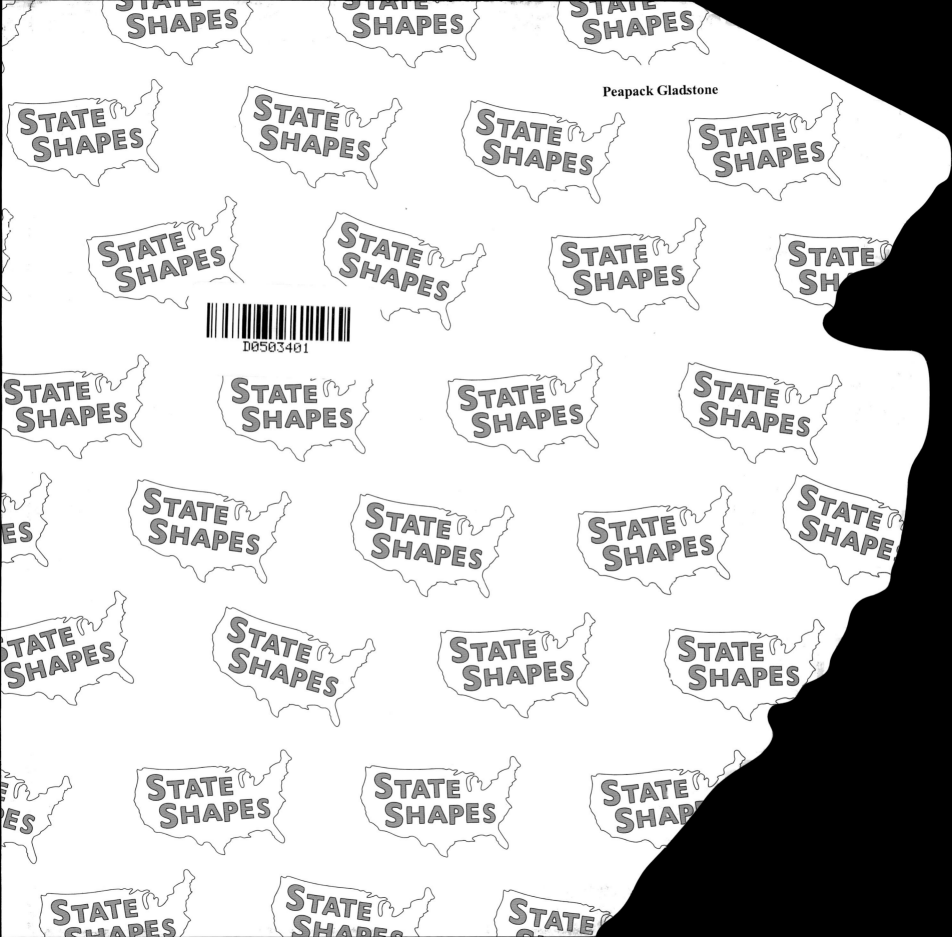

Peapack Gladstone

D0503401

State Shapes New Jersey
Text copyright © 2009 by Black Dog & Leventhal Publishers, Inc.
Illustrations copyright © 2009 by Alfred Schrier

Published by
Black Dog & Leventhal Publishers, Inc.
151 W. 19th Street
New York, NY 10011

Distributed by
Workman Publishing
225 Varick Street
New York, NY 10014

Manufactured in China

Cover and interior design by Sheila Hart Design, Inc.

ISBN-13:978-1-57912-820-3

h g f e d c b a

Library of Congress Cataloging-in-Publication Data
is on file at Black Dog & Leventhal Publishers, Inc.

STATE
SHAPES

NEW JERSEY

By

ERIN McHUGH

Illustrations by Alfred Schrier

BLACK DOG
& LEVENTHAL
PUBLISHERS
NEW YORK

PENNSYLVANIA

MARYLAND

VIRGINIA

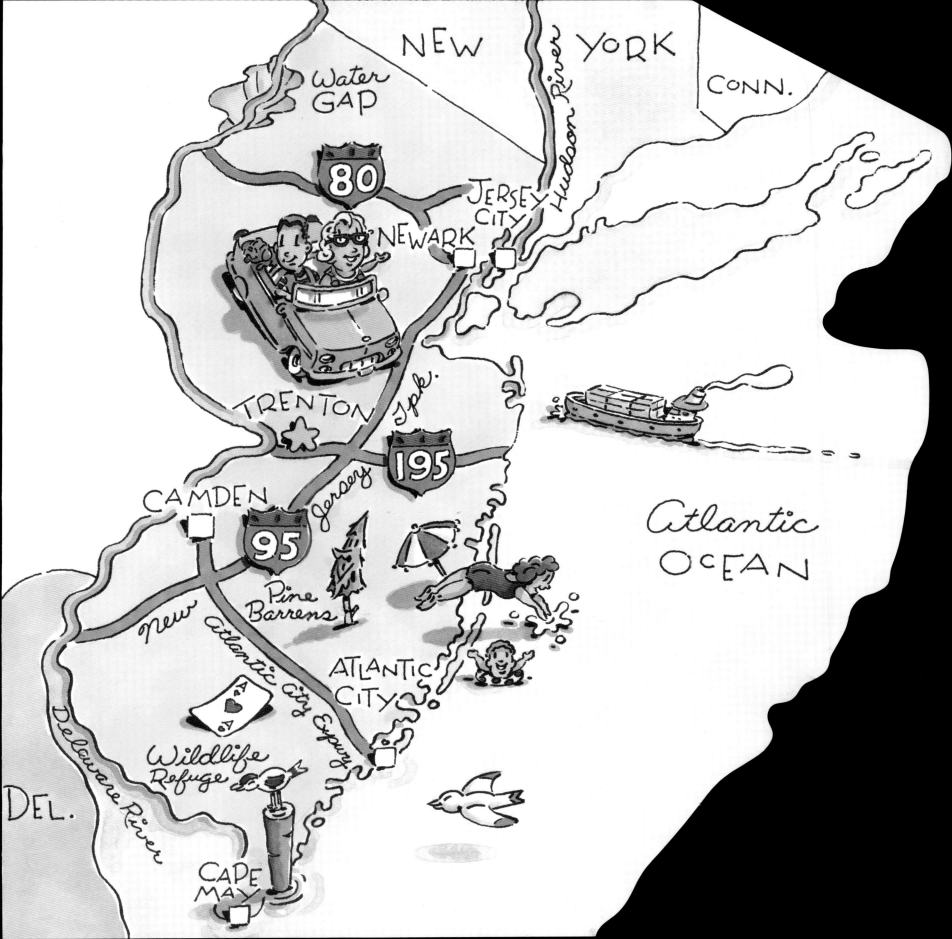

Hi, there! I like your red glasses. My name is Edward—I don't think I've ever seen you around here before.

My name is Sessalee, and you've never seen me because I just moved here to Maplewood last week from Texas. This is my new puppy, Barney. My dad named him after a lighthouse here.

That's funny! He must have been thinking of the Barnegat Lighthouse! Wow, Texas is really far down south. I've never been there. Is it hot there all the time?

Not always, but in the summer it sure is. I've never even seen snow before.

No way! We get a bunch here—sometimes we even get snow days off from school. But it gets hot in the summer, too. Maybe not as hot as Texas, but we spend a lot of time at the beach. And I'll bet you've never seen the leaves turn: it's called fall foliage, and it's beautiful.

Hmmm...maybe it's not so bad here after all!

Bad? New Jersey is great! We're just below New England, surrounded by New York, Delaware, Pennsylvania, and the Atlantic Ocean. I could show you all around if you want. It'll be fun. I can even bring you to the Barnegat Lighthouse!

I'd love that, Edward. Why don't you tell me a little bit about my new hometown first?

How did New Jersey get its name?

Maplewood? Well, my dad says it's what's known as a "bedroom community." That means that lots of the grown-ups here go into New York City to work, but come home here to live and sleep. Lots of towns around big cities are like that. But there are some cool things about this town.

Like what?

Well, way before the English settlers arrived, the Lenape Indians lived here. This was hundreds and hundreds of years ago, yet most of the main streets here in Maplewood were built on the original Indian paths. What's weird is that New Jersey is in the center of lots of the travel that goes on all over the East Coast. It's like the Lenapes knew how to map out everything, even way back then.

Cool. What else about Maplewood?

Well, there are two other sort of funny things that were invented here: the golf tee and Ultimate Frisbee.

Ultimate? Right here? I think I like it already.

There's plenty to like. How about we get started on our tour?

Yeah! Let's go!

A. It was named by the British after Jersey, the largest of the English Channel Islands. It was the third of the colonies to become a state in December 1787.

We're really close to New York City, aren't we? I'd like work there someday when I grow up.

Yup, we are, but New Jersey has a whole history of its own. The Lenapes lived here for thousands of years before this part of the United States had settlers. Giovanni da Verrazano, who was born in Italy but was exploring for the king of France, was one of the first Europeans to arrive—sailed up the coast from North Carolina. Verrazano made several stops in New Jersey as early as 1524, sailing around New York Bay, years and years before Henry Hudson did the same thing and got all the credit for discovering it!

So that's who the Verrazano Narrows Bridge is named after! Did Verrazano settle here in New Jersey?

Nope, he just kept sailing north, so it wasn't until the 1600s that people really came and built communities here, and they were Dutch, like Peter Minuet and the people that were living on Manhattan Island.

That's part of New York City.

Right. Swedish people and Dutch people were who lived in New Jersey way back then. In 1660, what's now called Jersey City became

Where was the first copper mined in the United States?

the first permanent city here—we'll stop by later. By 1664, the British were interested in all the great land and opportunities in North America, and declared that New Jersey belonged to them, taking it from the Dutch. For over twenty-five years the land was divided into East Jersey and West Jersey. And finally, in 1721, William Trent founded what was called Trent's Town.

I'll bet that's what's called Trenton now.

Yes, it is, and it's the capital of the state of New Jersey. Trent was actually a wealthy businessman, politician, and judge from Pennsylvania, and his house in New Jersey was just his country home.

That seems sort of weird—the first big city was named for someone from another state.

True, but in another way it's very much the way this state has always been. If you know about the Pilgrims coming to Plymouth, or the founding of Rhode Island, you know that religious differences played a big part in their early history. But from the very start, this state was open to all sorts of religions and people from many European countries. They all lived and worked side by side. New Jersey is still that way.

A. Right here in New Jersey, in a mine founded around 1640, in what's now Pahaquarry. It wasn't very successful, but another mine founded in 1712 produced enough copper to ship back to the Netherlands.

Hey, speaking of the Verrazano Bridge, can you tell me how many bridges and tunnels go from New Jersey to New York City?

Okay, not the Verrazano; even though he explored New Jersey, that bridge goes from Staten Island to Brooklyn, two boroughs of New York City. There's one bridge, right? And the Holland Tunnel!

Right, and one more tunnel: the Lincoln Tunnel. It goes from Weehawken to Manhattan, and was built in the 1930s. The Holland Tunnel was built in the 1920s and goes between Jersey City and Manhattan. The bridge is called the George Washington Bridge, and it goes to Manhattan from Fort Lee. It's one of the busiest bridges in the world.

New Jersey's kind of a weird shape, isn't it? It's so loooooonnng.

Hmmm...you're right. It seems like, when you look at the states that the British first came to along the East Coast, they're all odd shapes, with the state lines decided by wars or geography—like rivers and mountains. Lots of the states out west look square, like they were divided by a ruler.

What famous sporting event took place in New Brunswick?

Probably by the time the ones out west became states, the government decided where the borders would be.

Pardon me, I'm lost! Can you help me find Morristown?

WEIRD NEW JERSEY

Good point, Sessalee. Let's see if I can tell you some other interesting stuff about my—I mean, our—state. Lots of people believe that there are plenty of ghosts, strange stories, and scary people, places, and things here. So many that two guys publish a magazine called *Weird New Jersey* that talks about just this kind of stuff!

Cool! Tell me something scary.

My favorite thing is that New Jerseyites have seen plenty of UFOs. From crazy lights over Morristown in 1947, to a real flying saucer–shaped one over Passaic in 1952, to a night in 2009 when a bunch of different people—a pilot, even!—saw one over Morristown again.

I totally believe in UFOs. And now I'm glad my dad didn't move us to Morristown!

A. The first intercollegiate football game ever. It was played in 1869 between Rutgers and Princeton. Princeton won.

So all these bridges and tunnels cross over the Hudson River, right?

Yup. You probably know it was named after Henry Hudson, who sailed his boat, the *Half Moon*, up the river, looking for a way to India through a place everyone called the Northwest Passage. Of course, once again, our friend Verrazano really discovered the Hudson, since he found New York harbor, which is the mouth of the Hudson River. There was no way he was going to find the Northwest Passage near New Jersey—you'd have to go above Canada to do that!

The Hudson is really pretty—what are those big cliffs?

Those are called the Palisades. In some places they're 550 feet tall! The Lenape Indians said they were "rocks that look like rows of trees," and they do. That's also where the name Weehawken came from, and that's the town we're in now. The Palisades go north from here up the Hudson for about 20 miles, and in the Palisades Interstate Park you can hike and everything.

There's also a really famous historical event that took place here: a duel!

Q. Where did the word cliffhanger come from?

What? Duels aren't real—
they're just in old movies.

Not this one. And they were really
famous people, too. Politicians!

No way!

Totally way. It was 1804, and the
duel was between Alexander Hamilton,
the very first secretary of the treasury (and the
guy who is still on a ten-dollar bill) and Aaron Burr, who was Thomas Jefferson's vice
president, and had just lost the election for governor of New York. They had been enemies for
a long time, not only about politics, but personal things, too. Burr insisted that Hamilton had
said terrible things about him during his political campaign, and Hamilton wouldn't apologize.
So Burr challenged him to a duel—duels were just beginning to be outlawed in many states—
and he shot Alexander Hamilton and killed him. Now
two statesmen were gone: one through death,
the other by a damaged reputation. It was a
very dark moment in American politics.

That is a crazy story. No
wonder duels were outlawed!

A. From the Palisades, of course!
They were used as a background
for gripping scenes in an early silent movie series
called "The Perils of Pauline."

This place is awesome! Where are we? There's the Statue of Liberty right in front of us. And what's that other island with all the other old buildings?

That's a lot of questions, Sess! For starters, that's Ellis Island, where boats full of immigrants from all over the world used to land, full of people who left their country for a better life in America. You know how on the base of the Statue of Liberty it says, "Give me your tired, your poor, your huddled masses yearning to breathe free"? Well, Ellis Island is where they went.

I'm confused. I thought both those islands were part of New York State.

You're not the only one. For over a hundred years, New Jersey and New York have been arguing which state they belong to, and it's harder to decide because they're islands, not attached to either state. It got complicated, but the short answer is that both states own some of both Liberty and Ellis Islands, and the National Park Service is sort of the boss of them both.

What state has the densest population?

14

C'mon, let's take the ferry! I want to climb up inside the statue, and then go to Ellis Island, too.

Good idea. On Ellis Island, you can see really interesting things about lots of the people who came here. Even kids like us!

And then I want to see the Liberty Science Center!

You've got plenty of energy! The Science Center in Jersey City has one of the best IMAX screens in the whole world, with great movies about bugs, or dinosaurs, and other science stuff. And they even do this thing called Live Science, where kids like us get to volunteer and join in on experiments and demonstrations. Lots of things here are what they call interactive, which means you get to take part, not just watch.

You can go on ahead, Edward. I'm going to stay here and watch this movie!

A. New Jersey! About 1,030 people live inside every square mile—that's thirteen times the national average.

You can't even tell here on the shore that Jersey City is the second-largest city in New Jersey; almost 250,000 people live here. It's always been an important port in our country's history, and companies often put their manufacturing plants and warehouses right here at the water's edge, so they don't have to ship things far away for the next step of their production.

I was wondering what all these buildings were—that makes sense.

Once Jersey City was part of a city called Bergen, but ferries to New York, railroads, and all the new immigrants who worked and lived here made it a place of its own, and it split off from Bergen and sort of annexed other nearby towns over time. It's a good example of how the Industrial Revolution arrived and made a city where nothing had been.

There seem to be plenty of cities right around here when I look at the map.

There are: Bayonne, Elizabeth, New Brunswick, and Perth Amboy, are all very close. Right now we're in another funnily named city: Hoboken!

Hoboken? As in "hobos"?

Well, maybe. Some people think they were named after the poor men who jumped on trains from here, riding off to other places across the country. No one is sure where the name of this town came from—maybe from the Dutch,

What kind if roadside restaurant is especially popular in New Jersey?

maybe from the Lenape language. But something totally awesome happened here way back in 1846. Guess what it was.

Guess? I have no idea! What?

The very first official baseball game took place here between the Knickerbocker Club and the New York Nine at Elysian Fields!

Right here? Wow—that is cool!

I know! It sort of makes sense. There really was no good place to play in Manhattan—it was already getting crowded—so they came over here. And that's sort of how Hoboken got popular in the first place: as a resort place for New Yorkers to come and relax in the early 1800s. Go Jersey!
And by the way, the Knickerbockers won, 23–1.

And I know one more thing about Hoboken: it's where Frank Sinatra grew up! He's one of the most famous singers and actors of all time.

Yep! Sinatra was the king of the Rat Pack—a bunch of really cool singers and actors who appeared together on stage and in films in the early 1960s.

A. The diner! There are more than six hundred statewide, considered to be the most of any one place in the world.

I've heard New Jersey called the Garden State—why is that, Edward? So far all we've talked about is cities!

Well, despite being densely populated, almost half of New Jersey is woodlands. It actually makes sense that New Jersey is called the Garden State. We grow a lot of flowers and produce here, and the odd shape of New Jersey looks a little like "an immense barrel." The story goes that a Jersey resident said that way back in 1876, and that it's filled to the brim with delicious things to eat, with New Yorkers grabbing from the top, and spilling out to Pennsylvanians at the other end. Look, it even says "The Garden State" on our license plates!

What kinds of food are grown here?

I think just about everybody agrees that the Jersey tomato is about the biggest, juiciest, most delicious tomato you can eat! But then we grow a lot of lettuce, corn, and cranberries, too, and a weird, fancy salad green called escarole. And here's a really funny thing: the seedless watermelon was first grown in New Jersey!

Yum! Except I do like to spit the seeds...

Me, too. We grow a lot of peaches, blueberries, and strawberries, too. And we make tons of dairy products, thanks to all our Jersey cows.

What two aviation firsts happened in Keyport, New Jersey?

Let me guess. The cows aren't named after New Jersey, but the Jersey Islands.

I know you're kidding, but in fact…you're right! I'll tell you one more of our delicious products that come from here, and it also comes from something living: honey! The honeybee is the New Jersey state insect.

Cool! I love honey on toast. Having a state insect is pretty funny, though. Do you have like a state tree and other stuff?

Oh, sure. Let's see: the flower is the violet, the tree is the red oak, the state animal is the horse, and you won't be surprised to hear the state fruit is the blueberry, and the vegetable is the Jersey tomato.

Wow! Those are a lot of official state symbols!

Yep! And right now I'm going to teach you how to do the state dance: the square dance!

A. Not only was the first seaplane built here, but the first airmail was from here, too. The mail went to Chicago!

Now we're going to stop by Newark—it's not the state capital, but it's the biggest city in New Jersey.

Newark grew fast, right from the start. We know the Pilgrims came to Plymouth in 1620, and by 1670 this city even had a hotel! And by 1680 there were already five hundred people living in Newark. Aaron Burr was born here, whom we just heard about fighting the duel.

As time went on, different ethnic groups began to pour into Newark because there was so much work during the time of the Industrial Revolution, when America started inventing and using machines to do a lot of its work. There were Irish and then German, then, early in the twentieth century, African Americans.

It looks nice here—there are so many new buildings!

Newark suffered some hard times in the mid-twentieth century, but has bounced back. It led the way politically by being the first big city in the Northeast to elect an African American mayor. And since the 1990s, you're right, there has been lots of construction: a science park; some big office buildings; an arts center; and a great park.

Would I know anybody famous who grew up here in Newark?

Yup–you beat me to it. Two of the most awesome people I can think of: Shaquille O'Neal and Queen Latifah!

Wow! I love them both, but especially the Queen.

What do dentures have to do with Newark?

Shaq's maybe my favorite basketball player ever. My mom says he's a great role model, too. Some athletes get all caught up in their fame, but Shaq is even a reserve police officer.

How cool. Say, what's that big stadium over there?

That's the Meadowlands. What you're seeing is a stadium, and both the New York Jets and the New York Giants play football there; I know that's sort of weird, since they're New York teams playing in New Jersey, but what can I say?

Here's where all the wide open space is! But also, the Meadowlands is about 8,400 acres of beautiful wetlands, with a whole ecosystem of its own, that's especially known for its great bird-watching. But before people started trying to take care of our environment, all kinds of toxic waste and everything else got dumped here. My grandfather says he remembers hearing that even parts of London that were destroyed in World War II were brought here.

That sounds like a real mess.

No kidding. But in the last few decades, everybody's been trying really hard to clean it up. Now there are trails to hike, and kayaking—you can even take boat tours.

A. Celluloid—the first plastic that was a commercial success—was made right here by John Wesley Hyatt. It was also used early on to make billiard balls and photo film.

That boat tour around the Meadowlands was so much fun! What other kind of great stuff is there that kids can do in New Jersey?

Plenty! First, there's all sorts of sports stuff to do, all year round. We do lots of skiing, and last winter I started to learn how to snowboard, too. My favorite thing to do in the summer is tubing down the Delaware. You can fish and canoe and all kinds of other cool outdoor stuff, too. My family likes to hike a lot.

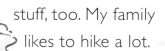

There's even a part of the Appalachian Trail in New Jersey, which goes all the way from Georgia to Maine. The New Jersey part is 72 miles, and our goal is to do it all, bit by bit: we've done 34 miles so far!

There's also a really unusual thing to do involving animals that you wouldn't believe.

Try me!

Okay. There's a place right near the tubing spot where you can go see packs of wolves.

No thanks.

Q. What was New Jersey the first in the Union to do on November 20, 1789?

It's not what you think, Sessalee, and it's not dangerous. It's what's called environmental tourism. At the Lakota Wolf Preserve, they have tundra, timber, and arctic wolves, and if you take a walk through, you'll see all kinds of other wildlife. Come on—we'll talk to the folks who work here: they know all about wolf packs and how these animals live, play, and even interact with humans. They raise and care for these wolves—you can even adopt one, though of course you don't get to take it home! Ahh-ooooooo!

They are beautiful—I've never seen one up close. Are there other parks in New Jersey that have normal stuff—like roller coasters?

You're kidding, right? You've never heard of Kingda Ka? Someday someone will probably build something higher, but right now it's the tallest steel roller coaster in the whole world!

I have gotta see this!

You'll love it! I was sort of chicken the first time: it's 456 feet high, and it's at this place called Six Flags Great Adventure. It goes 128 miles per hour—last year I went on it seven times in a row. We still can get two or three rides in before the sheep-shearing festival...

A. On that day, New Jersey ratified the Bill of Rights. That began the process of making the first ten amendments to the United States Constitution, the law of the land.

You know, I liked those wolves more than I thought I would. But did you say something about sheep sharing? What do they share, sweaters? Hahahaaa!

Hilarious, Sessalee, but it's sheep *shearing*, not sharing. A sheep's wool grows all winter long and keeps them warm, but in spring, it gets cut—or sheared—off, and then yes, plenty of sweaters are made. This shearing is in Hunterdon, and it is the largest in the whole eastern United States, where they do about five hundred sheep. They make a big festival of it—it's fun to watch, and they have music and a pig roast, people selling the crafts they make—all kinds of things. And guess what else? They make cheese from the sheep milk, too!

Wow. I'm starting to think New Jersey really is the coolest. What kind of things do people do for a living?

Lots of people go and work in New York City, of course, so that means lots of them work in industries that are big in Manhattan: banking and the stock market on Wall Street, making and designing clothes in the garment industry, and other businesses like advertising and book publishing are huge there.

What company did Thomas Edison form that is in the top 25 biggest companies in the world today?

Publishing! That's what I want to do when I grow up!

No way—me, too! I love to read. But there are other industries throughout the rest of the state. New Jersey is also one of the most important research centers in the world, so many of America's major companies have their headquarters here. There are telecommunications companies, big pharmaceutical—they make drugs and medicine— scientific companies and electrical equipment companies, too.

But there are two men who are big heroes of mine, and they both did most of their important work here in New Jersey. C'mon, I'm going to take you to Menlo Park.

A. General Electric! They are working very hard today on clean technology, to make the world a greener place.

I'm actually going to take you to two different towns and tell you about two great men: I mean these guys were so huge they changed the entire world. The first man invented so many things you're not going to even believe it. Do you know what a patent is?

Nope.

When someone invents something, they apply to the U.S. government to hold what's called a patent on their invention so no one can steal their idea from them. Well this man held a world record of 1,093 patents, including one for the lightbulb. Know who he is?

Of course—Thomas Edison! But I didn't know about all his other inventions.

Oh, sure. And though he later moved to West Orange, it all started right here. Part of the town was then called Menlo Park, and when Edison invented the phonograph, it seemed almost like magic to the public: that's how he got the nickname "the Wizard of Menlo Park."

Isn't a phonograph a record player?

That's right—a lot of kids don't know that. Before MP3s and CDs, there were record albums, played on a machine with a needle reading a disc. At first he made recordings on tinfoil way back in 1877, which could only be used a few times. But by 1912, phonographs were for sale everywhere, and recordings, too.

Q. What is unique about the Popcorn Park Zoo in Forked River, NJ?

Was that Edison's first invention?

Nope. The first big one was what's called a ticker tape machine. It was an electronic way of transmitting to the whole country the changing stock prices in New York.

Then he invented the lightbulb?

Well, he didn't invent the first lightbulb, but Edison invented the first practical version of what's called the incandescent lightbulb in 1879. And then, a dozen years later, he invented the motion picture camera.

You mean Thomas Edison was in the movie business? I didn't know that!

He sure was. He invented the Kinetoscope, a camera that would show objects in motion. Later he even built a studio here in New Jersey called the Black Maria, which most people call "America's first movie studio."

You know what? I'm putting Thomas Edison on my list of heroes, too.

A. It was founded by the Humane Society as a home for sick, injured, elderly, and abused animals, lots of them wild and exotic.

You wouldn't think two of the biggest geniuses of all time could live so close to each other, but they did. Now that we've learned about Edison, I'm going to show you where one of the greatest scientists of all time used to live. Have you ever heard of Albert Einstein?

The guy with the frizzy hair?

That's him. He's probably the world's most famous scientist ever. He studied physics. It's way complicated, but he figured out something called the theory of relativity, and it changed science forever.

And he lived in this little town?

Yes. It's called Princeton, and Einstein came here from Europe in the 1930s because he was Jewish. Adolf Hitler had come into power, and he didn't want any Jews in Germany.

That's discrimination!

It's a lot of what World War II was about. Before the war started, Einstein came here for a peaceful life where he could work, play his violin, and go sailing.

But before he moved to the United States, a lot of his work was about proving the existence of atoms. Everyone learns about atoms and molecules now by the time they're our age, but a hundred years ago, lots of scientists didn't even believe atoms were real. Einstein helped change that, and later urged President Franklin Delano Roosevelt to start work on the atomic bomb.

Q. What very famous person is buried in Princeton?

Wow, he was an important man! And this is where Princeton University is, right?

Right! One of the first colleges in the United States and one of the best—it's been around for over 250 years. Some really famous people went here, like F. Scott Fitzgerald, one of America's most famous writers; Meg Whitman, who started eBay; Jeff Bezos, who began Amazon.com; and even two presidents—James Madison and Woodrow Wilson.

I know another famous Princetonian— Michelle Obama!

You're right! But wait, I have to tell you one more thing about Einstein: when he died, they wanted to try to figure out why he was so much smarter than everyone else. So they took out his brain and studied it!

They did not!

Oh yes, they did! And there was a certain kind of cell that he had more of than most people. Also, it led some scientists to think that maybe peoples' brains are all built a little differently. That would explain why some people are better at one thing than another. Einstein himself said he thought more in pictures than in words.

You know what, Edward? You know a lot of weird stuff, and Barney and I like you already.

A. President Grover Cleveland (1837–1908). He is the only president in history to have served two terms not in a row. He was both the 22nd and 24th president of the United States!

Let me take you to Trenton now, which is the state capital. And I'll tell you something else kind of funny on the way about the New Jersey Turnpike.

What could be strange about a boring old highway?

The rest stops, that's what. Even though it's only 122 miles long, you almost have to get on it in order to get from the northeast United States to the South and other parts of the country. C'mon, see if you can figure out what's so odd about these stops.

Hmmm, let's see. Clara Barton, Walt Whitman, Joyce Kilmer—hey, these rest areas are all named after people. That is sort of nutty!

Yep! Anyway, Trenton played an important part during the Revolutionary War. New Jersey was called the "Crossroads of the Revolution"—296 battles happened here, more than in any other colony. You've probably seen that picture of George Washington standing up in the

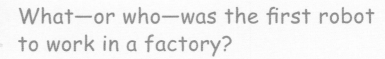
What—or who—was the first robot to work in a factory?

boat crossing the Delaware River, right? Well, he was crossing to Trenton! It was General Washington's first big victory. Even the last big battle of the revolution, the Battle of Springfield, took place here in 1780, when our soldiers held off the British who were headed to Morristown where there were lots of munitions. Trenton was even capital of the whole United States for a couple of months in 1784.

In the last century, Trenton went through some hard times, like so many other American cities, but lots of the state government is here because it's New Jersey's capital. In fact, the state of New Jersey is Trenton's largest employer. About 20,000 people here work for the State of New Jersey.

Say, let's go hang out in that park for a while. My feet hurt!

Good idea. Isn't this huge? It's called Cadwalader Park, and it's over 100 acres, right in the middle of Trenton. The man who designed it, Frederick Law Olmsted, also designed Central Park in New York City.

Oh, and a cool sports thing happened here: in 1896, the first professional basketball game was played, with the Trenton YMCA playing the Brooklyn YMCA. Trenton won 15–1.

Everyone got paid $15, except for one guy, who for some reason got paid $16.

Go, Trenton!

A. His name was Unimate, and he started his job at General Motors in Trenton in 1961.

Let's take a little spin through Camden. It's one of those American cities that was a busy, successful manufacturing town during the Industrial Revolution and through a lot of the twentieth century. But Camden suffered when factories closed, and people started moving out to the suburbs. Like there was a shipbuilding company here that used to be the busiest in the world. Lots of jobs are lost when a place like that closes. But there's one company that still here after all these years: Campbell Soup!

Now follow me, Sessalee, because I want to show you a special house. But first, let me tell you about something that was invented here that you hardly see anymore: the drive-in movie.

Hey, my grandma told me about those! They sound really neat!

Here is where it all happened. A man named Richard Hollingshead invented it in 1933. He experimented in his backyard by putting a movie projector on his car, and hanging a screen between two trees in his yard. Finally he opened a drive-in for real, with a snack bar in the back, and they because a huge thing all over America. Once people began to rent movies in their houses, drive-ins began to disappear. But they're so much fun that people are starting to build them again!

It's sort of funny all this movie and sound stuff happened near where Thomas Edison lived.

Hey, you're right—I never thought of that. There was one really famous man who lived here at the end of his life, and now his house is a museum.

What was the Victor Talking Machine Company?

His name was Walt Whitman, and he was an American poet. His most famous book of poetry is called *Leaves of Grass*. My sister is reading it at her high school.

I've heard of him! Does that sign over there say "aquarium?"

I was going to surprise you! Yup, the New Jersey Aquarium is here in Camden, too. How do you like sharks?

Not so much.

Well, guess what? At this aquarium, you can even swim with them!

That sounds crazy to me.

I've done it! They teach you to snorkel, and then you can swim nearby—it's not dangerous. Then you feed the stingrays yourself! Maybe you'd like the penguins better. You can go behind the scenes on Penguin Island with the biologists and learn all about them. Believe me, there's plenty of fun stuff here at the aquarium!

The aquarium itself seems almost as large as the ocean!

You know why? There are 8,000 animals here and two million gallons of water.

I'm not going to let you scare me away from swimming with the sharks. Lead the way!

A. Based in Camden in the early twentieth century, it made phonographs—called Victrolas— and phonograph records.

We're pretty far from New York City now. Where are all the woods you talked about?

Funny you should ask. Down here in southern New Jersey are the Pine Barrens.

What's that?

It's a really thick forest that covers over a million acres of land. It became the country's first national preserve in 1978, and even more than the Meadowlands, there's like an entire biosphere of various plants and stuff in here.

Bass River State Forest is also right here in the Pine Barrens— it's even got a 50-mile trail through it. You can camp, hike, swim, and everything. Also there's a place called Batsto Village near here that has an old general store, sawmill, and gristmill: it was an old glassmaking and iron center in the state during the eighteenth and nineteenth centuries.

Okay, Sessalee. Are you ready for one more incredibly scary thing? About the Jersey Devil? And I don't mean the hockey team!

Um...not really.

C'mon, you gotta hear this. For hundreds of years, people have been saying there's a creature in the Pine Barrens called either the Jersey Devil, or the Leeds Devil, after a lady in the 1700s who said if she had

Q. What huge sports "first" happened in 1995?

a thirteenth child it would actually be the devil. Folkore says the baby was born normal, but then turned into a creature with hooves, a tail, and wings, with a head like a horse. Since then, tons of people have reported seeing it!

Nooo, Edward!
I don't believe it!

Ha, ha. Maybe it doesn't exist.
Or maybe it does!
Okay, maybe you'll like
this better. How about going to the rodeo?

That's more like it! We have tons of those in Texas. I love the rodeo.

Then I'll bet you're glad you won't have to miss them up North. The Cowtown Rodeo had been going on for over seventy-five years, and it's right near here. They have bull riding and steer wrestling, calf roping and bareback bronco riding—all the things you've seen out West. In fact, Cowtown in the oldest weekly rodeo in the United States, and you can go every Saturday night in the summer.

A. The New Jersey Devils, the state hockey team, won the Stanley Cup. It was the first time any New Jersey professional sports team won a major title championship ever!

Hey, remember I told you before about the Lenape Indians who were here before the colonists? Now that we've done the cowboy thing, we could also go to a powwow if you'd like.

Oh, boy—really? That was something I thought I would never see again after leaving Texas.

Not to worry! It's right near the rodeo in Salem County, and will have everything you remember: dancing, drums, and all the great food and Native American crafts.

You know what, Edward? Suddenly I'm not homesick at all anymore.

New Jersey's great, isn't it? Some other interesting historical things have taken place here, too.

Tell me one.

In 1937, there was an accident at the Lakehurst Naval Air Station everyone still calls the *Hindenburg* disaster. The *Hindenburg* was a gigantic German airship—a little like the blimps you sometimes see

What is a huge business in New Jersey that doesn't make an actual product?

over football games on TV—that carried people from Europe to America. Airships were a pretty new idea, and the *Hindenburg* had already made seventeen trips across the Atlantic the year before. It took three whole days to cross the ocean!

But this time something terrible happened—no one is sure even today what it was, but many things made it highly flammable, and just a few moments before it was to land, it burst into flames. Lots of the passengers on board were killed.

That's a horrible story!

Sometimes a disaster teaches us lessons and moves technology forward; the *Hindenburg* disaster, like the sinking of the *Titanic*, was one of them.

But there's another great flight story that happened in 1793 in nearby Gloucester County. A Frenchman named Jean-Pierre Blanchard delivered the first airmail letter there to George Washington all the way from Philadelphia—in a balloon!

I've read about him! Didn't he invent the parachute, too?

You're right! He was one cool dude.

A. Tourism! People coming here for fun and vacation makes it New Jersey's second largest industry.

Say, speaking of flying, didn't Charles Lindbergh live in New Jersey?

Lucky Lindy, they called him! He may be the greatest pilot who ever lived. He was just a guy who just flew an airmail plane, but in 1927 he flew this flimsy little airplane he called *The Spirit of Saint Louis* all alone, non-stop from Long Island all the way to Paris, France. Everyone thought it was impossible, but Lindy showed them! You can still see Lindbergh's plane at the National Air and Space Museum in Washington, DC.

He was as famous as a rock star. Lindbergh was an inventor, too, and one of the things he helped develop was an artificial heart pump—in those days heart surgery of any kind was not usually successful. He was also an environmentalist, and was one of the first to talk about saving the whales.

It sort of sounds like New Jersey was first to do a lot of things. What else?

Q. Where is the first national historic park in the country?

Oh, all kinds of stuff. How about a few—I guess I wouldn't call them transportation things, but they are ways to getting places. Let's see…in 1824, a guy from Hoboken named John Stevens invented a steam locomotive that could actually pull a train along a track. Later, John Holland built the first submarine commissioned by the navy; it launched in 1900. He also had patents for submarine guns and a special kind of propeller—this dude was awesome! These first submarines were tiny, only about 50 feet long!

Okay, and one more. In 1919, the first airplane flight carrying passengers flew from New York City to Atlantic City—and believe me, it wasn't like the comfortable flights we have today! It was like a noisy warplane.

Wow. Those are important firsts. Hey, isn't Atlantic City where that boardwalk is?

Yup, and I'm going to take you there soon. Wait until you see all of New Jersey's beautiful beaches.

A. The Morristown National Historic Park was created in 1933. More than twelve thousand soldiers had slept on its grounds in makeshift cabins during a bitter cold winter of the Revolutionary War.

There's plenty of fun to be had all along the Jersey Shore, but there is a special stop I always like to make.

Oh, brother. Now what?

No, you'll love this! It's the Jersey Shore Pirates!

Is that another sports team?

No, silly, it's an adventure for kids! We'll climb aboard the Sea Gypsy, find sunken treasure, fight other pirates, shoot water cannons, and even get tattoos and learn how to speak pirate lingo.

Arggh! Avast and ahoy!

That's the spirit! Blackbeard and Captain Kidd both sailed these waters, and they were real pirates. C'mon, let's go! I'm a swashbuckler!

There are lots of beaches and different communities to visit along the Jersey Shore. Did you ever seen the world's scariest shark movie, *Jaws*? Believe it or not, it was based on some real shark attacks way back in the summer of 1916.

No way!

Way! Don't be afraid though, Sess. You should always be careful of the ocean, of course, but the

Q. **What sweet confection was invented at the Jersey Shore in the 1870s?**

beaches are so pretty and we're going to have a ball! Besides, if we're lucky we might see one of the greatest rock legends of all time. Keep your eyes peeled.

Hey, wait—we're in Asbury Park. Everybody knows that's where Bruce Springsteen is from!

You got it! This town got sort of run down in the last century, like a lot of the Shore towns, but they're all really coming back, with loads of things on the boardwalk being fixed up. Also, it's known as one of the Shore's prettiest beaches. There's a big rock-and-roll scene here, and when we get old enough, we can even go to the famous Stone Pony, where so many bands got their start. The Boss still goes there!

The boss of what?

Bruce Springsteen, Sessalee! That's his nickname.

Duh, Edward. I knew that—I was just teasing! Everyone knows no one loves Jersey like The Boss.

Let's go have Barney's picture taken at his lighthouse, and then off we'll go!

 Saltwater taffy!

Tell me more about Barney's lighthouse.

Actually, there are eleven lighthouses you can visit in the state. I know you said your dad named him after a lighthouse, but Barney's probably named after a whole bunch of stuff in New Jersey. The lighthouse is named after Barnegat Peninsula, which is what's called a "barrier island." If you look at this map, you see it's a long skinny piece of land that separates the mainland of Ocean County from the Atlantic Ocean.

Oh, I see. And the water between the island and the mainland is even called Barnegat Bay!

Let's face it: Barney's famous!

Hey, on our way to the beach, tell me some more things that were "firsts" in my new home state. I need to get my mind off that scary Jersey Devil!

Ha! Okay, let's see…Here are some electronic facts. In 1883, Thomas Edison proved he could light an entire town by electricity by hanging wires overhead and using a generator. The village of Roselle lit up like a Christmas tree, astonishing everyone.

WHAT TOOK YOU SO LONG?

Q. **What is Hadrosaurus foulkii?**

42

Then there was Les Paul from Mahwah, who any guitarist will tell you was the awesomest dude ever. He invented one of the first electric guitars way back in the 1930s—even Eric Clapton plays a Les Paul guitar! And then he went and invented multitrack recording!

New Jersey is like Electric World! Are we getting near Atlantic City now? I'll bet I know something you don't about a certain board game and Atlantic City.

You mean boardwalk. Atlantic City—or AC, as some people call it—had the first one in the country, built way back in 1870.

You can walk on it forever. It's 4½ miles long!

Nope. That's not what I'm talking about. If you look at a Monopoly game, you'll see all the streets are named after real places in Atlantic City!

I didn't know that, but I get it now. That's why you can buy hotels in Monopoly, too—there are plenty of hotels in Atlantic City. Loads of casinos, too. My grandma likes to come and play the slots. But my dad likes blackjack.

A. It's the name of the first dinosaur found in the United States, in 1858 in Haddonfield, NJ. Nearly the whole skeleton was here, so it helped convince people there really had been such a thing as dinosaurs in the past.

You know, the Jersey Shore is huge, and is has plenty more than just where we've visited. I told you how important tourism is to our state, and lots of it is people coming here, especially in the summer. It's 90 miles long—that's as far as Philadelphia is from New York City! My family goes to Ocean Beach, but there are towns all up and down the coast, and they're all different from the other.

I love it here—so many people and old hotels and everything. Can we finally go to the beach and take a swim? You keep promising!

Well, our tour of New Jersey is almost over, so I thought I'd take you all the way to the tip of New Jersey to the beach in Cape May, one of the most beautiful in the whole country. It's the oldest seaside resort in the country, too, from the early 1800s. That's why all the houses are so pretty. They sort of look like birthday cakes, don't they?

Yeah, and some are such funny colors. But why are so many people are carrying binoculars?

Cape May is the best place to watch birds. People come to see more than four hundred kinds of birds migrate. And there are the cool ferries that take you to Delaware and their beaches. And then there's one more special kind of boat trip: whale watching!

Q. What is the New Jersey state bird?

I've always wanted to do that—let's go do that,
and then, finally, a swim at the beach!

You're on. Whale watching is one of my favorite things to do.

To tell you the truth, it's even more exciting than
the pirate ship! New Jersey is awesome, Edward.
I'm so glad you saved Cape May for last.
Barney and I are going
to love it here,
especially with
a good friend
like you.

C'mon, last one
in the water buys the
ice cream!

A. The Eastern goldfinch,
which sports a bright yellow
breast.

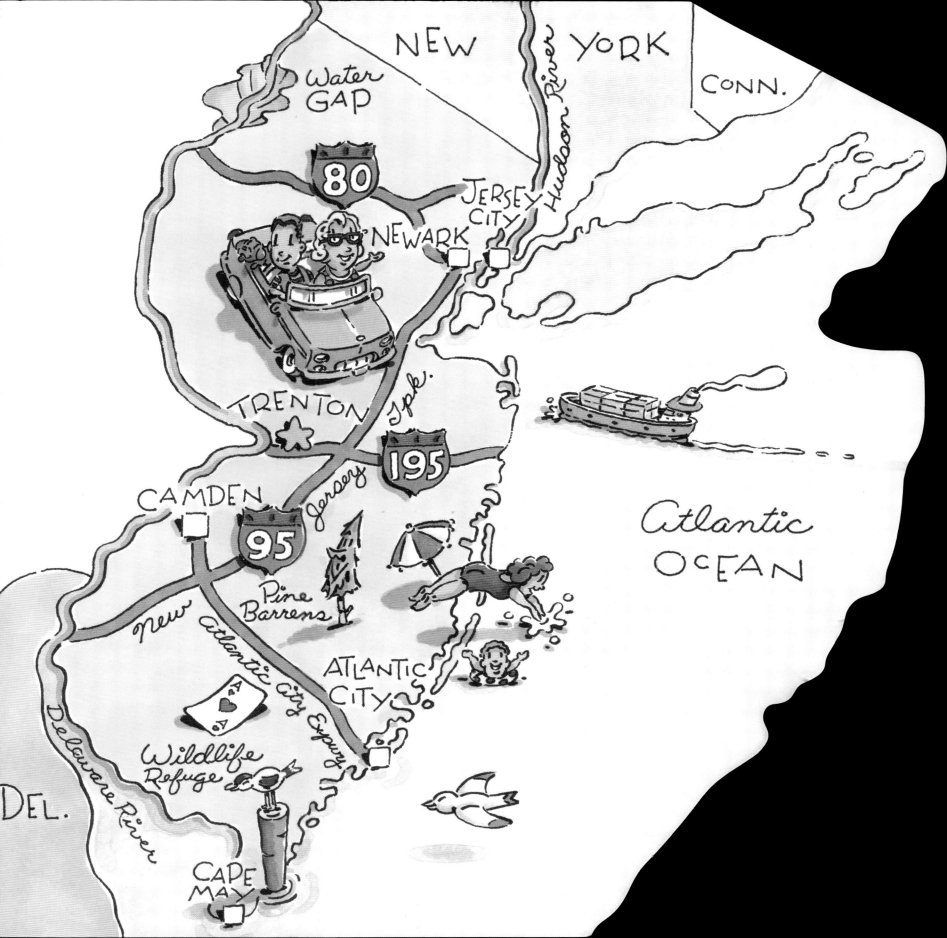

STATE SHAPES